THE COMPLETE KETO DESSERTS COOKBOOK FOR CARB LOVERS

Owen Moss

CONTENTS

INTRODUCTION

Let's face it – dieting and healthy eating is not the easiest thing in the world! I know it perfectly well since I have tried various low-calorie diets and restrictive eating plans over the past years. In the best-case scenario, I have found that I gained the weight back. In general, I felt miserable because I failed again. I damaged my metabolism so I experienced frequent hunger which led me to weight gain and so on and so forth. Then, I took one step further and tried to consume fewer and fewer calories, while increasing the time spent working out. Things went from bad to worse. I have struggled with tiredness and a lack of energy; I have fallen into the starve-binge cycle and put my health in danger. What I missed most were sweets. However, it is well known that you cannot eat desserts on a weight loss diet, so I wholeheartedly accepted that rule. I thought it was good for me and my body, but as it turned out, I was wrong. I couldn't escape from my own personal hell – cycles of restriction, binge, despair, and guilt. It can be very frustrating!

There are different beliefs that you can lose some pounds by eating this or avoiding that. If only it were that easy! Consuming fewer calories does not automatically lead to weight loss. Everybody is different and there is no such thing as one-size-fits-all. I realized – there is no only one simple formula such as "calories in vs. calories out" that will make miracles for me! Moreover, the researchers have found that everyone responses differently to the same food because of different gut bacteria. Then, it also depends on your basal metabolic rate, health condition, DNA, and ultimately your lifestyle. There is a considerable amount of information out there, so learning what makes your own personal diet plan can be difficult. What type of food should you eat to supply your body with essential nutrients? It has been said that a well-balanced diet is the key component that contributes to a healthy lifestyle. The human body needs six major types of nutrients: carbohydrates, protein, fats, vitamins, minerals, and water.

I finally realized that I need a comprehensive diet plan that works for me. A plan that consists of all types of food including desserts. Fortunately, I healed my relationship with food and found a diet plan that finally worked for me. I discovered a ketogenic diet! Basically, this diet includes consuming mostly good-quality protein (meat, fish, and eggs), as well as low-carb veggies, healthy fats and oils, nuts, seeds, and some dairy products. On a diet, hardly anyone thinks about desserts, right? The ketogenic diet is different – desserts and treats are allowed on the ketogenic diet! Moreover, there are desserts you will not believe are actually keto-friendly. It sounds too good to be true! I know, I was skeptical too. Luckily, I was proven wrong because keto-friendly desserts are better than I thought.

The Ketogenic Diet in a Nutshell

The concept behind the ketogenic diet is simple – It is a low-carb dietary regimen. Your goal should be to get more calories from high-quality protein and good fats than from sugars. Your macronutrient ratio should fall into the following ranges: 60-75% of calories come from fat, 15-30% of calories from protein and 5-10% of calories should come from carbohydrates. If you eat less than 40 grams of carbs on a daily basis, you can turn your body into a fat-burning machine. It is incredibly easy to start a keto diet, since the list of foods we are allowed to eat is long. You can eat above ground vegetables, non-starchy foods, good fats, nuts, meat, fish, seafood, and some fruits. The best part, though, we can eat a dessert occasionally. During such a diet, there are foods you can eat freely, other food that you can eat in moderation and there are also foods that are off-limits.

If your diet includes lots of carbohydrates, your body will produce a lot of glucose; then, it will use glucose for fuel or the main source of energy. Consequently, excess fat will be stored in your body rather than burned for energy. What actually happened to your body on a ketogenic diet? If you follow the conventional Western diet, the carbohydrates are turned into glucose so the body uses them for energy. On the healthy ketogenic diet, when you get a small number of calories from carbohydrates, stored fat is divided into two major organic compounds – fatty acids and ketones. Consequently, your body is "forced" to builds up ketones and use them as the main energy source. The state that occurs when you have a lot of ketone bodies in your blood is known as "ketosis". This a natural process that occurs when your food intake is lower than usual (during starvation, fasting, prolonged exercise, or a low-carb diet). Your body is intelligent and it will soon adapt to the state of ketosis that can stimulate fat breakdown and reduce your appetite; consequently, you will be able to lose excess fat. In addition, the ketogenic diet mostly focuses on foods that may speed up metabolism and encourage weight loss. They include protein-rich foods (such as fish, eggs, and poultry), nuts, seeds, cacao, vegetables, spices, tea, and coconut oil.

What you can eat on the ketogenic diet?
Here is the list of keto-friendly foods for you to get an idea of what to consume:
Organic poultry – whole chicken, turkey, duck, and goose.
Organic meat – pork, beef, veal, goat.
Fish & Seafood – fat fish, shrimp, crab, lobster, mussels, scallops, clams, squid, and oysters.
Plain dairy products – Greek-style yoghurt, cheese, crème fraîche, mascarpone, full-fat sour cream, heavy whipping cream.
Eggs – hard-boiled, fried, deviled, poached, and scrambled.
Vegetables – non-starchy (above-ground) broccoli, cauliflower, cucumber, asparagus, tomatoes, Brussels sprouts, pepper, greens, zucchini garlic, etc. Canned and pickled veggies are allowed, just be careful about added sugar.
Fats & Oils – avocado, butter, ghee, olive oil, coconut oil.
Nuts – most of them and nut butter (preferably homemade, plain and unsweetened).
Fruits – berries, apples, plums, and citrus fruit.
Herbs and spices – fresh or dried.
Baking ingredients – keto flour, baking powder, baking soda, unsweetened dark chocolate, unsweetened cocoa, glucomannan powder, and pure vanilla extract.
Keto-friendly beverages – plain water, tea, coffee, sparkling water, keto smoothies. As for alcohol, good options include whiskey, vodka, rum, brandy, and tequila.
Vegetarian options – tofu, tempeh, full-fat plant-based milk, nutritional yeast, and seaweed.

What you can't eat on the ketogenic diet?

This list includes grains, grain-like seeds, flours (wheat flour, cornmeal, cornstarch, cassava), rice, beans, all types of sugar and syrup, processed vegetable oils, factory-farmed meat, starchy vegetables, and fruits. This is pretty acceptable to me. So, you probably already know that sugary drinks, processed food, and junk food are fattening; in addition, they may hide sodium, sugar, preservatives, and dangerous levels of chemicals. However, there are pretty "innocent" foods that are strongly associated with weight gain and health problems. They include canned goods, processed meat, deli meats, soybean oil, fatty conventional red meat, coffee creamers, sugar-sweetened beverages, and energy drinks. In fact, food nutritionists avoid these foods so you should too.

Should you track your calorie consumption?

As a unit of energy that our body uses to perform daily tasks, calories are important. Generally speaking, when you consume excess calories over a longer time period, your body will store them as fat; on the other hand, if you take in fewer calories, you will lose weight. Basically, I try to stay within my daily calorie needs. However, this is not the whole story. Each of the macronutrients provides a different amount of energy. Fat as the most calorie dense macronutrient produces 9 calories per gram; protein – 4 calories per gram; carbs: 4 calories per gram. In other words, calories count but they are not all equal. Calories are important but rather than counting them choose keto-friendly foods that reduce appetite and regulate hormones. Experts also recommend watching the amount of cholesterol in your food. Eating nourishing and well-balanced diet is the best way to provide your body with essential nutrients and lose weight in the process. As you can see, the ketogenic diet is easy to follow as long as you stick to some general rules.

What are the benefits of the ketogenic diet?

There are a great number of benefits of the ketogenic diet. Significant weight loss is one of the most obvious benefits. The ketogenic diet has been proven to affect appetite-regulating hormones. In addition to boosting your metabolism and helping you lose weight, following a keto diet has been shown to provide significant health benefits. They include better mental focus and cognitive functions, reduced inflammation, and lower blood sugar. If you eat healthy fats, you can improve heart health and prevent cardiovascular diseases while significantly reducing bad cholesterol. Moreover, studies have shown that a keto diet may help reduce the risk of cancer and balance hormones. This can be particularly helpful in women with PCOS (Polycystic ovarian syndrome, which is a typical endocrine disorder).

Seeds, nuts and avocado contain good, unsaturated fats that can help your body to lower triglycerides. Cutting out sugars can also reduce insulin levels in your body. It has proven beneficial in treating metabolic syndrome and epilepsy. Besides being beneficial for your health, the ketogenic diet can increase your energy levels. In fact, your body has to break down fat instead of carbs. Studies have proven that the ketogenic diet can increase your mental performance and concentration, since your brain breaks down ketones as the main energy source.

One of the Biggest Myths About Weight Loss

Why we crave sweets? There is the science behind cravings for comfort foods. In fact, it is all happening in your brain or more precisely in the regions that are responsible for memory, reward, and pleasure. In other words, sugar craving is linked to reward-seeking behavior that is memorized in your hippocampus. Some experts claim that the body craves sweets because it lacks certain nutrients. Further, hormone imbalance may cause sugar cravings. There is the possibility of a connection between sugar cravings and pre-menstrual syndrome and pregnancy when you are more likely to reach for simple carbohydrates like pastries, chips or sweets. Did you know that poor night's sleep can cause serious sugar addiction? Stress may trigger emotional eating and sugar cravings. Many people use sweets to cope with certain situations and suppress emotions. Maybe not surprisingly, your diet can cause cravings too. If your diet plan includes lower-quality foods, low-protein and low-fat intake, your blood sugar will rise rapidly and boost the hormone insulin, causing abnormal blood lipids too; your brain needs quick energy boost and subsequently, you'll be wanting more and more simple sugars. Cravings for sugar may be a need for certain nutrients such as magnesium or iron. The keto diet is one of the most effective ways to stop or reduce food cravings since it doesn't allow sugars that don't exist naturally in the foods. The keto diet focuses on high protein intake, preferably from good-quality sources such as organic meat, fish, seafood, and pasture-raised eggs. Science has proven that plenty of protein can help reduce sugar cravings, without pushing us over the calorie edge. If you generally eat a keto diet or any diet that is low in added sugars, you will be safe. To sum up, if you have abnormal and unusual sugar cravings you should consider the biological and psychological reasons behind that behavior. Otherwise, if you have normal sugar cravings periodically, you can eat dessert and still lose weight.

Why you should eat dessert?

Avoiding dessert and labeling it as off-limits can lead to mental problems, according to science. Restrictive diets almost always have the opposite effects. Ironically, if you're trying not to think about desserts, you may even find yourself thinking about sweets all the time. You may end up daydreaming about a huge chocolate cake. For many people, avoiding the sweets they want may make their cravings even worse. This can lead to overeating and emotional stress.

When you enjoy a portion-controlled treat whenever you want, you will eat mindfully and ditch the guilt that causes stress and anxiety. Believe me, if you decide to enjoy dessert now and then, you'll be satisfied with fewer portions such as a small square of chocolate or a healthy protein smoothie. This approach will help you control your obsession with sweets. That sounds clichéd, but eating a balanced diet is the key to the ideal weight and overall health. Therefore, you should eat a healthy dessert not sugary desserts with "empty" calories. Numerous studies have found that eating dessert can help you eat less calories on a daily basis. What nutritionists eat for dessert? Their go-to dessert choices include dark chocolate, nuts, nut butter, fruits, and homemade energy bars.

Have a Sweet-Tooth and Stay Fit

So, you reached your ideal weight. What now? Here are a few tricks you might not know. I maintain my ideal weight for years by simply rotating low-carb days with higher carb days. It works for most people, including me, so you can try this method too. A typical week may consist of three low-carb days, two moderate-carb days and two high-carb days. You can add more protein i.e. more calories to your meals while keeping your carbs low. Further, you can eat a little more carbs only before and after a workout. Once you lose weight, you should go slowly and raise your daily carb intake by 10 - 20 grams during the next two weeks. Your body needs time to adapt to new BMI. In this phase, opt for nutrient-dense food such as potatoes and bananas and avoid processed food. In fact, real food will satiate your taste buds and help you feel fuller; consequently, you will eat fewer calories. Further, you can try LCHF, Paleo, or low-carb Mediterranean diet. You can combine your diet with intermittent fasting and muscle-gaining programs, too. The secret is to find that perfect diet and workout plan that work for your lifestyle, age, body type, and activity level. Yes, sure you can eat dessert and still be healthy and fit. There are so many pitfalls, but you can learn to avoid them along the way. Trust me, I did it.

Quick and easy dessert ideas. There are many great ideas for having your dessert and staying in ketosis. A refreshing yogurt parfait with nuts and some shaved keto chocolate is ideal for dessert or snack. It is healthy and loaded with heart-healthy ingredients. In general, Greek yogurt will work wonders as a protein-packed, low-calorie base for your favorite desserts such as fruit salads, frozen yogurt, ice pops, or yogurt bark. If you like creamy cakes, switch them out for a piece of cheesecake. A peanut or sesame butter in combination with fruits are sweet enough to stop sugar cravings; just make sure to avoid super-sweet fruits such as figs, bananas, canned and dried fruits. A smoothie with full-fat milk, peanut butter and some berries makes a great breakfast or dessert; not only it can satisfy your sweet teeth, but it also provides a good serving of protein and fiber; you can freeze leftovers and indulge in great popsicle treats later. An avocado and cacao mousse makes a great go-to snack for you and your kids. Other guilt-free options include flavored Greek yogurt, frozen yogurt, sorbet, hot chocolate, and dark chocolate. A homemade chocolate bar is actually my favorite go-to dessert because I can bring it with me wherever I go – to work, to the gym, on travel, etc. The intensity of unsweetened chocolate makes it easier for me to be satisfied with a small portion.

Balance your diet. Opt for a healthy main course (for instance, choose grilled meat instead of fried fish, and a nutrient-dense side dish instead of chips). Later, you can treat yourself with dessert.

Drink lots of water. Some experts claim that dehydration can cause sugar cravings. Next time you crave that chocolate, drink a glass of water and wait a minute or two. After that, you will eat a small, healthy dessert instead of big piece of the pie.

Eat mindfully. When you feel the urge to dig a spoon into that chocolate cake with butter-cream frosting, step back and find a healthier way to satisfy a sweet tooth. Do not let those little treats ruin your hard-earned results with the ketogenic diet. Try eating fresh fruits such as berries; they are nature's candy and they can fill your cravings in most cases.

Listen to your body. You should recognize your main diet pitfalls such as liquid calories, extreme calorie reduction, skipping meals, stressing out about your diet, turning to emotional eating.

Reduce, don't eliminate desserts. Think about cutting your favorite dessert in half. Avoid sneaky liquid calories in cocktails and sodas and you are more likely to take off these pounds. Share your dessert with your dining companion. I can't explain but eating dessert with my partner just tastes better.

Eat fiber-rich food. Fiber is one of the key nutrients that keeps you full longer. If you're trying to shed some pounds, fiber is a must!

Indulge in a keto dessert for breakfast. According to recent studies, eating a "dessert breakfast" may help you speed up weight loss. First and foremost, it will reduce your sugar cravings. Then, your metabolism is most active in the morning. And last but not least, you will regulate ghrelin hormone ("hunger hormone") levels.

Go workout. Exercise is one of the most important components of a healthy lifestyle, according to science. You should be exercising at least 3 times per week. To live an active lifestyle, you do not have to go to the gym; simply try to incorporate exercise into your daily routine. Some fun things you can do include going for a walk, taking the stairs, playing with kids and pets, gardening, cycling, and so forth. Eat a good post-workout dessert to help with recovery; opt for high-protein foods such as whey protein, eggs, protein bars, nuts, peanut butter, chia seeds, and avocado.

Finally, yet importantly, in addition to a well-balanced diet, there are a few additional habits that may contribute to your health. They include moving, cooking at home, taking vacation, taking time for yourself, and good night's sleep. If you are looking for healthy ways to indulge your sweet tooth, this recipe collection may be your go-to source for the healthiest desserts ever.

Tips for the Best Keto Desserts Ever

It is not easy to come up with a healthy dessert, especially if it is a low-carb one. At first, it is difficult when putting in practice. Here are a few tips to make your keto desserts less boring.

- It's amazing what a pinch of aromatics and few drizzles of lime juice can do to jazz up a dessert and the whole diet. Don't be afraid to experiment with spices such as nutmeg, cinnamon, star anise, and vanilla.
- On the keto diet, I love using fresh lemon and orange juice. I often use the rinds in my desserts. So, do not throw the lemon peel away; grate the lemons you are planning to use for juice and freeze them for later use.

- Pour the water into the jar; add whole lemons to the jar and place them in the refrigerator. Your lemons will yield much more juice.
- For the perfect cheesecake, place the baking pan in a rimmed baking sheet. Add some water to the baking sheet and bake your cheesecake as you normally do.
- Whipped cream turned out watery? No problem, pour it into the chilled metal bowl and transfer the bowl to the freezer for 30 minutes before using. Immediately, beat your cream with an electric whisk until stiff peaks form. To prevent this situation, I like to dissolve 1 teaspoon of gelatin in a little bit of water; then, I beat the gelatin mixture into my cream.
- If your recipe calls for egg whites, you can save the yolks in the refrigerator for up to two days. Keep them, unbroken, in a bowl covered with cold water.
- To save lots of time, have the most common dessert ingredients on hand and use store-bought, already made ingredients. Baking in multiple batches can save your time in the kitchen, too. If you are not in a hurry, make your own desserts from scratch. I love baking my own desserts and storing leftovers for later. When a craving hits, I can always indulge in a low-carb, guilt-free dessert.
- Simplify your desserts. This recipe collection is chock-full of easy-to-follow, delectable recipes so you will enjoy making and tasting them. Your enjoyment is the key to success!

- **How to stock a pantry for the best keto desserts?**

Here are my best hacks on how to stock a keto pantry. It includes my pantry staples and a few words about them.

Keto-friendly sweeteners

Erythritol is a zero-carb sweetener. Stevia and Monk fruit are zero carb sweeteners too but they have certain health benefits. Pure, organic Stevia has no impact on blood sugar levels, according to science. Monk fruit has anti-inflammatory and antioxidant properties. Splenda (sucralose-based sweetener) contains 0.5g of carbs per packet of 1g while xylitol contains 4 grams of carbs per 1 teaspoon.

Keto-friendly flours

Low-carb flours can help you re-create your favorite desserts and fit them into your diet plan. The best keto flours include almond flour, coconut flour, psyllium husk flour, cricket flour, ground flax seeds, ground chia seeds, and ground sunflower seeds. They are high in fiber and omega-3 fatty acids; in addition, some of them such as chia seeds contain 0g net carbs per serving. Oat fiber is perfect for baked goods since it contains 3 grams of carbs per 100 grams of product and they all come from fiber.

Coconut oil

When it comes to keto desserts and baking, coconut oil makes a great substitute for unhealthy shortenings such as margarine and hydrogenated oil. You can replace butter with coconut oil with a 1:1 ratio. Pro tip: always use room-temperature ingredients in combination with coconut oil. When it comes to the other fats for your favorite desserts, you should avoid processed vegetable oils and trans fats. Bad fats include vegetable shortening, margarine, corn oil, soybean oil, cottonseed oil, and safflower oil.

Cocoa powder

For me, one of the hardest things to give up is chocolate. The good news is that cacao powder is full of antioxidants; it can lower your blood pressure and protect your heart. The best part – cocoa and dark chocolate can keep you feeling fuller for longer. Therefore, you don't have to avoid chocolate, you need to make a few simple tweaks. Use unsweetened cocoa powder, raw cacao nibs, sugar-free cacao butter, and dark baker's chocolate.

Nuts and Seeds

Along with avocado and coconut oil, nuts and seeds contain good-for-you fats. The best options include pecans and Brazil nuts (they contain 4 grams of carbs per 100 grams or 3.5 ounces), macadamia nuts (5 grams of carbs per 100 grams), walnuts and hazelnuts (7g of carbs per 100g), peanuts (8g of carbs per 100g), and almonds and pine nuts (9g of carbs per 100g). However, if you're aiming to lose weight, keep in mind that nuts contain lots of calories. Go nuts!

A Word about Our Recipe Collection

My grandma used to say, "There's nothing a good cake can't solve." These recipes come from home cooks, my mom and my grandma. I mixed their immense cooking wisdom with my knowledge about keto diet and nutrition, and Voila! Even if you managed to lose weight as a short-term goal, keep in mind that being healthy involves more than a healthy BMI (Body Mass Index). You should find a realistic and sustainable eating plan that suits your needs in your day-to-day life. My goal with this cookbook is to help you to jumpstart your weight loss and develop healthy eating habits. I want to inspire you to eat well and make the best keto desserts that everyone is excited to have on their table.

This collection combines old-fashioned, classic recipes with innovative and cool dessert recipes. You can start with foolproof desserts such as chocolate-avocado mousse and fat bombs and then, you can experiment with keto ingredients. This collection with 75 fail-safe recipes will be your go-to source for convenient, affordable, and delectable keto desserts – from classic family recipes and timeless Christmas treats to the most popular trendy desserts that kids love! These desserts are not only suitable for romantic candlelight dinners, but they can also save your busy mornings.

The recipes consist of the ingredients list, estimated cooking time and temperature, easy-to-follow directions, and nutritional analysis. If you are looking for healthy desserts to enjoy on your keto diet, this recipe collection with 75 delectable recipes is exactly what you need. Bon appétit!

1. Chocolate Almond Ganache Cake

(Ready in about 50 minutes + chilling time | Servings 10)

INGREDIENTS

1/2 cup water
3/4 cup granulated Swerve
14 ounces unsweetened chocolate chunks
2 sticks butter, cold
5 eggs
1/2 teaspoon pure almond extract
1/4 teaspoon ground nutmeg
1/4 teaspoon ground cardamom
A pinch of salt

For Almond-Choc Ganache:
3/4 cups double cream
9 ounces sugar-free dark chocolate,
   broken into chunks
1/4 cup smooth almond butter
A pinch of salt
1/2 teaspoon ginger powder
1/2 teaspoon cardamom powder

DIRECTIONS

- Begin by preheating your oven to 360 degrees F. Line a baking pan with parchment paper.
- Now bring the water to a rolling boil in a deep pan; add the Swerve and cook until it is dissolved.
- Microwave the chocolate until it melts. Add the butter to the melted chocolate and beat with an electric mixer.
- Add the chocolate mixture to the hot water mixture. Now, add the eggs, one at a time, whipping continuously.
- Add the almond extract, nutmeg, cardamom, and salt; stir well. Spoon the mixture into the prepared baking pan; wrap with foil.
- Lower the baking pan into a larger pan; add boiling water about 1 inch deep.
- Bake for 40 to 45 minutes. Allow it to cool completely before removing from the pan.
- Meanwhile, place the double cream in a pan over a moderately high heat and bring to a boil. Pour the hot cream over the dark chocolate; whisk until the chocolate has melted.
- Add the remaining ingredients for the ganache and whip until it is uniform and smooth. Finally, glaze a cooled cake and serve well-chilled. Enjoy!

Per serving: 313 Calories; 30.7g Fat; 5.5g Carbs; 7.3g Protein

2. Ultimate Raspberry Cheesecake Bars

(Ready in about 30 minutes | Servings 6)

INGREDIENTS

For the Cheesecake Bars:

1 stick butter, melted

4 eggs

1 cup mascarpone cheese

1 teaspoon vanilla paste

1/4 teaspoon star anise, ground

3 tablespoons Swerve

1/3 teaspoon baking powder

For the Raspberry Topping:

3/4 cup, frozen raspberries

1 ½ tablespoons erythritol

1/2 teaspoon lemon juice

A pinch of salt

1 ½ tablespoons water

DIRECTIONS

- Thoroughly combine all ingredients for the cheesecakes with a hand mixer. Line a baking pan with parchment paper or Silpat mat.
- Bake in the preheated oven at 330 degrees F, approximately 25 minutes. Transfer to a wire rack to cool completely.
- Meanwhile, place all of the ingredients for the topping in a pan that is preheated over a moderate heat; bring the mixture to a boil.
- Now, reduce the heat and let it simmer until the sauce has thickened.
- Cut the cheesecake into squares. Spoon about 2 tablespoons of the raspberry sauce over each cheesecake square. Enjoy!

Per serving: 333 Calories; 28.4g Fat; 6.3g Carbs; 11.7g Protein

3. Coconut Chocolate Candy

(Ready in about 15 minutes + chilling time | Servings 16)

INGREDIENTS

1 ½ cups bittersweet chocolate, sugar-free, broken into chunks

4 tablespoons coconut, desiccated

1/2 stick butter

1 cup double cream

3 tablespoons xylitol

1/2 teaspoon pure almond extract

1 teaspoon vanilla paste

A pinch of salt

A pinch of freshly grated nutmeg

1 tablespoon cognac

1/4 cup unsweetened Dutch-processed cocoa powder

DIRECTIONS

- Thoroughly combine the chocolate, coconut, butter, double cream, xylitol, almond extract, vanilla, salt, and grated nutmeg.
- Microwave for 1 minute on medium-high; let it cool slightly. Now, stir in the cognac and vanilla.
- Place in your refrigerator for 2 hours. Shape the mixture into balls; roll each ball in cocoa powder and enjoy!

Per serving: 90 Calories; 7.3g Fat; 2.9g Carbs; 3.7g Protein

4. Chocolate Swirl Meringue Cookies

(Ready in about 1 hour + chilling time | Servings 7)

INGREDIENTS

7 egg whites

1/3 teaspoon cream of tartar

A pinch of coarse sea salt

1 ¾ cups Swerve granular sweetener

1/4 teaspoon ground cloves

1/2 teaspoon ground cinnamon

1/2 teaspoon vanilla paste

1/4 cup cocoa powder, unsweetened

DIRECTIONS

- Whip the eggs with an electric mixer. Mix in the cream of tartar, increase the speed to high and continue mixing until the egg whites form soft peaks.
- Mix in the salt and slowly add the Swerve, mixing continuously until the Swerve is dissolved.
- Fold in the ground cloves, cinnamon, vanilla, and cocoa powder. Continue whipping until the mixture becomes whipped to the desired stage. When firm peaks form, the mixture should not be beaten any longer.
- Drop the egg mixture by teaspoonfuls onto a lightly greased cookie sheet. Bake in the preheated oven at 225 degrees F for 55 minutes or until your meringues are dry and stiff. Turn the oven off; let your meringues sit in the oven for 1 hour.
- Let your meringues cool on wire racks. Store at room temperature.

Per serving: 71 Calories; 4.5g Fat; 2.6g Carbs; 6.1g Protein

5. Chocolate Mousse with Orange

(Ready in about 15 minutes | Servings 4)

INGREDIENTS

2 egg yolks

3/4 cup heavy cream

3 ounces Ricotta cheese, at room temperature

1 tablespoon freshly squeezed orange juice

1 ½ teaspoons orange zest

1/2 teaspoon ground cinnamon

1/4 cup granulated stevia erythritol blend

1/4 cup unsweetened cocoa powder

DIRECTIONS

- Beat the egg yolks with your electric mixer until thick and pale.
- Heat the cream in a pan over medium heat. Gradually stir the hot cream into the egg yolk mixture.
- Turn the heat to low and cook for about 5 minutes, stirring constantly, until your mixture has thickened.
- Now, beat the remaining ingredients with your electric mixer until everything is creamy.
- Fold this mixture into the cream mixture and serve well chilled.

Per serving: 154 Calories; 15g Fat; 5.1g Carbs; 5.3g Protein

6. Old-Fashioned Mocha Cobbler

(Ready in about 50 minutes + chilling time | Servings 12)

INGREDIENTS

Batter:

1 cup almond meal

1 cup coconut flour

A pinch of table salt

1 teaspoon baking powder

1/2 cup granulated Swerve

1/2 teaspoon almond extract

2 eggs

1 stick butter, at room temperature

1 teaspoon fresh lemon juice

1/3 cup full-fat milk

1/2 cup hot brewed coffee

Filling:

12 ounces Mascarpone cheese, softened

1/4 teaspoon orange flower water

1/3 cup granulated Swerve

DIRECTIONS

- Thoroughly combine the almond meal, coconut flour, salt, baking powder and Swerve. Mix in the almond extract, eggs, 1 stick of butter; beat the mixture with an electric mixer.
- Slowly and gradually, mix in the lemon juice, milk, and coffee; mix until everything is well incorporated. Scrape half of the batter into a parchment-lined baking pan.
- Mix the ingredients for the filling in another bowl; mix until it is well combined. Distribute the filling over the batter as evenly as possible. Add the other half of the prepared batter.
- Bake at 320 degrees F for 40 to 43 minutes or until the top springs back when touched lightly. Transfer to a wire rack before chilling in the refrigerator. Serve well chilled.

Per serving: 233 Calories; 20.6g Fat; 4.6g Carbs; 1.6g Protein

7. Old-Fashioned Vanilla Cupcakes

(Ready in about 30 minutes + chilling time | Servings 8)

INGREDIENTS

For the Cupcakes:

3 tablespoons coconut oil

10 ounces Ricotta cheese, at room
    temperature

1 tablespoon rum

2 eggs

2 packets stevia

1/8 teaspoon ground cloves

1/4 teaspoon ground cinnamon

1/8 teaspoon nutmeg, preferably freshly
    grated

For the Frosting:

1/2 cup confectioners' Swerve

1/2 stick butter, softened

1 teaspoon vanilla

1 ½ tablespoons full-fat milk

DIRECTIONS

- Preheat your oven to 360 degrees F; coat muffin cups with cupcake liners.
- Thoroughly combine the coconut oil, Ricotta cheese, rum, eggs, stevia, cloves, cinnamon and nutmeg in your food processor.
- Scrape the batter into the muffin tin; bake for 13 to 16 minutes. Now, place in the freezer for 2 hours.
- In the meantime, combine the confectioners' Swerve with the butter and vanilla with an electric mixer.
- Slowly pour in the milk in order to make a spreadable mixture. Frost the chilled cheesecake cupcakes. Bon appétit!

Per serving: 165 Calories; 17.6g Fat; 3.4g Carbs; 5.2g Protein

8. Chocolate Blueberry Truffles

(Ready in about 15 minutes + chilling time | Servings 10)

INGREDIENTS

1 cup freeze-dried blueberries

1 stick butter

1 cup coconut oil

4 ounces unsweetened chocolate, roughly chopped

1 teaspoon vanilla crème stevia

DIRECTIONS

- Crush the dried blueberries with a pestle and mortar until you get a powder consistency; reserve.
- Heat a pan over a moderate heat; melt the butter, coconut oil, chocolate and vanilla crème stevia, stirring continuously.
- Now, transfer the chocolate mixture to a parchment-lined baking sheet.
- Sprinkle the blueberries and gently press them down into the melted chocolate. Swirl with a knife and transfer to your freezer.
- Let them cool and harden completely before breaking into pieces.

Per serving: 334 Calories; 37g Fat; 4.1g Carbs; 1.6g Protein

9. Coconut Dreamsicle Fudge

(Ready in about 15 minutes + chilling time | Servings 10)

INGREDIENTS

1 cup cocoa butter

1/4 cup coconut oil

1/4 cup butter

1/2 teaspoon ginger powder

1/2 teaspoon pure vanilla extract

1/2 teaspoon pure coconut extract

1 teaspoon Stevia

2 dashes of rum

DIRECTIONS

- Microwave the cocoa butter, cocoa oil, and butter until melted. Stir in the remaining ingredients and mix to combine well.
- Scrape the mixture into a parchment-lined baking pan; let it cool completely at room temperature.
- Then, place the baking pan in your freezer for a couple of hours. Cut into 1-inch squares and serve. Bon appétit!

Per serving: 250 Calories; 28.7g Fat; 0.2g Carbs; 0.6g Protein

10. Garden Mint Jelly

(Ready in about 45 minutes | Servings 10)

INGREDIENTS

2 envelopes unflavored gelatin

5 tablespoons Swerve

1 teaspoon peppermint oil

1 teaspoon pure vanilla essence

3/4 cup boiling water

1 ¼ cups heavy cream

DIRECTIONS

- Combine the gelatin, Swerve, peppermint oil, and vanilla extract in a heatproof dish.
- Pour in boiling water and stir well until the gelatin is dissolved.
- Stir in the heavy cream; whisk to combine well. Pour the mixture into paper cups sprayed with a nonstick cooking spray.
- Place in your refrigerator for 30 minutes or until they are firm. Unmold before serving and enjoy!

Per serving: 56 Calories; 5.5g Fat; 0.4g Carbs; 1.5g Protein

11. Hazelnut Shortbread Cookies

(Ready in about 15 minutes | Servings 12)

INGREDIENTS

1 stick butter, room temperature
1/2 cup Erythritol
1 large-sized egg
1/2 teaspoon rum extract
1 teaspoon coconut extract
1 cup almond meal

1 cup coconut flour
1 teaspoon baking powder
A pinch of sea salt
A pinch of freshly grated nutmeg
1 cup hazelnuts, chopped

DIRECTIONS

- Whip the butter with the Erythritol until light and fluffy. Fold in the egg and continue beating until everything is well incorporated.
- After that, stir in the rum extract and almond extract; mix again.
- In another bowl, thoroughly combine the almond meal, coconut flour, baking powder, salt, and nutmeg; mix to combine. Stir the butter mixture into the flour mixture.
- Afterwards, stir in the chopped hazelnuts and gently mix the dough; be careful not to overmix.
- Coat the bottom of a cookie sheet with parchment paper. Drop the dough by rounded tablespoonfuls onto the prepared cookie sheet (about 2 inches apart).
- Bake in the preheated oven at 360 degrees approximately 11 minutes. Bon appétit!

Per serving: 148 Calories; 14.9g Fat; 2.7g Carbs; 2.5g Protein

12. Nutty Coconut Crème Caramel

(Ready in about 40 minutes + chilling time | Servings 4)

INGREDIENTS

1 cup coconut cream, unsweetened

4 eggs

1/2 cup peanut butter

1/2 cup granulated Swerve

1/4 teaspoon ground mace

1/2 teaspoon pure vanilla extract

1/2 teaspoon pure almond extract

DIRECTIONS

- Begin by preheating your oven to 340 degrees F. Place 4 ramekins in a deep baking pan. Pour boiling water to a depth of about 1 inch.
- In a saucepan, bring the coconut cream to a simmer. In a mixing dish, whisk the remaining ingredients until the eggs are foamy.
- Slowly and gradually pour the egg mixture into the warm coconut cream, whisking constantly.
- Spoon the mixture into the prepared ramekins and bake for 35 minutes, or until a tester comes out dry.
- Allow it to cool about 4 hours. Can be stored in refrigerator up to 3 days. Bon appétit!

Per serving: 304 Calories; 29.7g Fat; 5.1g Carbs; 11.6g Protein

13. Dolci di Noci with Chocolate

(Ready in about 30 minutes | Servings 10)

INGREDIENTS

1 stick butter

1/2 teaspoon pure almond extract

2 eggs

15 drops liquid stevia

1/8 teaspoon kosher salt

1 ¾ cups almond flour

1/2 teaspoon baking powder

1/4 teaspoon ground cinnamon

1/2 cup walnuts, chopped

1/3 cup sugar-free baker's chocolate, cut into chunks

DIRECTIONS

- Heat the butter in a pan that is preheated over a moderate flame; stir and cook until it is browned.
- In a mixing bowl, beat the pure almond extract with the eggs, stevia, and salt.
- Add the melted butter, along with the other ingredients.
- Preheat your oven to 350 degrees F. Line a cookie sheet with a parchment paper. Spritz with a nonstick cooking spray.
- Bake for 25 minutes and transfer to a wire rack to cool before serving.

Per serving: 157 Calories; 17.8g Fat; 3.5g Carbs; 4.5g Protein

14. Chocolate-Covered Strawberry Jellies

(Ready in about 20 minutes + chilling time | Servings 8)

INGREDIENTS

4 (1-ounce) envelopes gelatin

6 fluid ounces water

6 ounces double cream

4 teaspoons liquid Stevia

1/2 cup strawberries, mashed

1 tablespoon brandy

6 ounces unsweetened bakers' chocolate, chopped

DIRECTIONS

- Mix the gelatin with the water and let it dissolve.
- Then, heat the double cream in a saucepan over a medium-low flame. Bring to a simmer and add the dissolved gelatin to the saucepan; stir with a wire whisk until well combined.
- Remove the saucepan from the heat. Add in the Stevia, mashed strawberries, and brandy.
- Pour your jelly mixture into the cake pan and refrigerate for 3 hours or until set. Cut your jelly into 1-inch squares.
- Microwave your chocolate until it fully melts (a candy thermometer should read about 120 degrees F).
- Next, dip the gelatin squares into the melted chocolate. Enjoy!

Per serving: 261 Calories; 19.1g Fat; 4.4g Carbs; 15.5g Protein

15. Tangy Blueberry Meringues

(Ready in about 2 hours | Servings 10)

INGREDIENTS

3 large egg whites, at room temperature

1/2 teaspoon vanilla paste

A pinch of salt

1 teaspoon finely grated lemon zest

1/3 cup Swerve

3 tablespoons freeze-dried blueberry, crushed with a pestle and mortar

DIRECTIONS

- Preheat an oven to 200 degrees F.
- Now, beat the egg whites, vanilla, salt, and lemon zest with an electric mixer on medium-high speed. Add the Swerve and continue mixing on high until stiff and glossy.
- Add the crushed blueberries and mix until everything is well incorporated.
- Drop the meringue, about 2 inches apart, on the parchment-lined baking sheets; you can use a pastry tube here.
- Bake about 2 hours. Leave the meringues in the turned-off oven for several hours.

Per serving: 51 Calories; 0g Fat; 4g Carbs; 12g Protein

16. Italian-Style Coconut Crème

(Ready in about 10 minutes + chilling time | Servings 6)

INGREDIENTS

4 ounces coconut oil

4 ounces coconut cream

2 teaspoons butter, softened

1 teaspoon instant espresso powder

3 tablespoons confectioners Swerve

A pinch of salt

1 teaspoon pure vanilla extract

DIRECTIONS

- Melt the coconut oil in a double boiler over medium-low heat.
- Add the remaining ingredients. Remove from the heat; stir until everything is well combined.
- Pour into a silicone mold and freeze overnight. Bon appétit!

Per serving: 218 Calories; 24.7g Fat; 1.1g Carbs; 0.4g Protein

17. Rustic Walnut Cupcakes

(Ready in about 30 minutes | Servings 10)

INGREDIENTS

1/3 cup butter room temperature

1/3 cup cocoa butter, softened

1/2 cup granulated Swerve

1/2 teaspoon pure almond extract

1/2 teaspoon pure vanilla extract

1 egg

1/4 cup walnut flour

A pinch of salt

1/4 teaspoon ground cardamom

1/4 teaspoon ground cinnamon

1/4 teaspoon ground star anise

2 tablespoons ground flax seeds

2 tablespoons ground chia seeds

1/4 cup cricket flour

1/3 cup coconut flour

1/2 teaspoon baking soda

1/2 teaspoon baking powder

4 ounces unsweetened baker's chocolate, broken into chunks

DIRECTIONS

- In a mixing bowl, thoroughly combine the butter, cocoa butter, and Swerve until well incorporated.
- Mix in the almond extract and vanilla. Slowly add in the egg and continue beating until well mixed.
- Gradually, stir in the walnut flour, salt, cardamom, cinnamon, star anise, flax seeds, chia seeds, flour, baking soda, and baking powder.
- Spoon the batter into a lightly greased muffin tin. Bake in the preheated oven at 360 degrees F for 10 minutes.
- Meanwhile, microwave the chocolate chunks until it fully melts (a candy thermometer should read about 120 degrees F).
- Drizzle the melted chocolate over each cookie and enjoy!

Per serving: 240 Calories; 24.4g Fat; 3.4g Carbs; 4.1g Protein

18. Mom's Ice Cream

(Ready in about 10 minutes + chilling time | Servings 4)

INGREDIENTS

1 ¼ cups almond milk

1/3 cup whipped cream

17 drops liquid stevia

1/2 cup peanuts, chopped

1/2 teaspoon xanthan gum

DIRECTIONS

- Combine all of the above ingredients, except for the xanthan gum, with an electric mixer.
- Now, stir in the xanthan gum, whisking constantly, until the mixture is thick.
- Then, prepare your ice cream in a machine following manufacturer's instructions.
- Serve directly from the machine or store in your freezer.

Per serving: 305 Calories; 18.3g Fat; 4.5g Carbs; 1g Protein

19. Mini Chocolate Cheesecake Cupcakes

(Ready in about 25 minutes | Servings 12)

INGREDIENTS

7 tablespoons butter, melted

5 eggs

2 ounces cocoa powder

1 teaspoon pure vanilla extract

1 teaspoon maple flavor

1/3 teaspoon baking powder

6 ounces Neufchatel cheese, at room temperature

1/4 cup xylitol

DIRECTIONS

- Beat all ingredients with an electric mixer.
- Place a paper baking cup in each of 12 muffin cups. Fill each cup 2/3 full.
- Bake at 360 degrees F about 23 minutes. Allow your cupcakes to cool completely; frost as desired and serve.

Per serving: 147 Calories; 14.5g Fat; 3.3g Carbs; 4.6g Protein

20. Key Lime Mousse

(Ready in about 10 minutes + chilling time | Servings 6)

INGREDIENTS

2 eggs, well whisked
1 egg yolk, well whisked
10 ounces fresh key lime juice
1 heaping tablespoon key lime zest

1 ½ cups Swerve
A pinch of salt
1 stick butter, softened

DIRECTIONS

- Whisk the eggs in a pan that is preheated over a moderate flame.
- Stir in the remaining ingredients and cook for 6 minutes more, whisking constantly.
- Turn the heat to low and continue whisking 2 minutes longer. Remove from the heat.
- Cover with a plastic wrap and chill overnight. Serve chilled and enjoy!

Per serving: 180 Calories; 18.6g Fat; 4.2g Carbs; 2.8g Protein

21. Sweet Tea Cupcakes with Vanilla Buttercream

(Ready in about 25 minutes | Servings 6)

INGREDIENTS

1/2 cup buttermilk
4 tablespoons coconut oil, at room
   temperature
1 large egg
1/2 cup Xylitol
1/3 cup sour cream
2 teaspoons Earl Grey tea leaves,
   ground
1/2 cup almond flour
1 tablespoon chia seeds, ground
1/2 teaspoon baking powder
1/4 teaspoon ground star anise
1/4 teaspoon ground cardamom
1/8 teaspoon grated nutmeg
A pinch of salt

Vanilla Bean Buttercream:
1/2 stick butter, at room temperature
1 vanilla bean, seed scraped
1 cup Xylitol
2 tablespoons heavy cream

DIRECTIONS

- Line a standard cupcake pan with paper liners and set aside.
- Mix the buttermilk, coconut oil, egg, Xylitol, and sour cream until well combined.
- In another mixing bowl, thoroughly combine the Earl Grey tea leaves, almond flour, chia seeds, baking powder, star anise, cardamom, nutmeg, and salt until well mixed.
- Now, add the flour mixture to the buttermilk mixture and mix again to combine well. Fill the cupcake liners. Then, bake in the preheated oven at 360 degrees F for 18 to 20 minutes.
- To make the vanilla bean buttercream, combine all ingredients in the bowl of an electric stand mixer. Mix until you achieve the desired consistency. Frost your cupcakes and enjoy!

Per serving: 247 Calories; 24.8g Fat; 3.9g Carbs; 4.1g Protein

22. Chocolate and Nut Balls

(Ready in about 40 minutes | Servings 12)

INGREDIENTS

1/2 cup almonds

1/3 cup walnuts

1/2 cup cashew butter

1/2 stick butter

2 tablespoons cocoa powder, unsweetened

10 drops liquid stevia

1 teaspoon vanilla extract

1/4 cup unsweetened peanut flour

DIRECTIONS

- Chop the almonds and walnuts in your food processor.
- Transfer to a mixing bowl; add the other ingredients.
- Scoop out tablespoons of batter onto a cookie sheet lined with a wax paper.
- Place in your freezer approximately 30 minutes. Store in your refrigerator up to 1 week.

Per serving: 114 Calories; 10.6g Fat; 3.4g Carbs; 3.1g Protein

23. Butterscotch Pecan Fat Bombs

(Ready in about 15 minutes | Servings 10)

INGREDIENTS

1/3 cup full-fat milk

1 cup Swerve confectioners

1 stick butter, room temperature

A pinch of sea salt

1 teaspoon butterscotch extract

1/2 cup pecans, chopped

DIRECTIONS

- Start by preheating your oven to 350 degrees F. Line a baking sheet with parchment paper.
- Mix all ingredients until well incorporated. Then, scrape the mixture on the prepared baking sheet; spread into a thin sheet.
- Bake in the preheated oven for 10 minutes; allow them to cool completely. Your fat bombs will harden as they cool. Bon appétit!

Per serving: 120 Calories; 12.8g Fat; 1.1g Carbs; 0.8g Protein

24. Chocolate Caramel Macchiato Truffles

(Ready in about 10 minutes + chilling time | Servings 8)

Per serving: 145 Calories; 13.8g Fat; 4.2g Carbs; 0.9g Protein

INGREDIENTS

3 tablespoons cocoa butter

3 tablespoons butter

3 ounces dark chocolate, sugar-free

1 teaspoon cold brew coffee concentrate

1 teaspoon sugar-free caramel flavored syrup

6 drops liquid stevia

DIRECTIONS

- Microwave the cocoa butter, butter, and chocolate for 1 minute or so.
- Stir in the remaining ingredients. Pour into candy-safe molds. Refrigerate until hard. Enjoy!

25. Cocoa and Almond Candy Melts

(Ready in about 10 minutes + chilling time | Servings 8)

INGREDIENTS

8 ounces Mascarpone cheese, room
   temperature
4 tablespoons cocoa butter
2 tablespoons sesame butter (tahini)
1 teaspoon liquid Stevia
1 cup double cream

A pinch of grated nutmeg
1/2 teaspoon ground cinnamon
1/4 teaspoon ground cloves
1 teaspoon rum extract
1/2 teaspoon almond extract

DIRECTIONS

- Mix the Mascarpone cheese with the cocoa butter and sesame butter; add the liquid Stevia and mix to combine well.
- Now, fold in the double cream; mix until it is combined well. After that, stir in the nutmeg, cinnamon, cloves, rum extract, and almond extract; mix well to combine.
- Using a small cookie scooper, place the mixture into mini-muffin paper cups. Eat at room temperature and enjoy!

Per serving: 145 Calories; 13.2g Fat; 4.5g Carbs; 0.9g Protein

26. Homemade Chocolate with Hazelnuts

(Ready in about 25 minutes | Servings 8)

INGREDIENTS

4 ounces cacao butter

1 tablespoon extra-virgin coconut oil

8 tablespoons cocoa powder

1/4 cup Swerve

1/4 teaspoon hazelnut extract

1 teaspoon pure vanilla extract

1/8 teaspoon coarse salt

1/4 teaspoon grated nutmeg

1/2 cup roasted hazelnuts, chopped

DIRECTIONS

- Melt the cacao butter and coconut oil in a microwave for 1 minute or so.
- Now, stir in the cocoa powder, Swerve, hazelnut extract, vanilla extract, salt and nutmeg.
- Pour the mixture into an ice cube mold. Add the roasted hazelnuts and place in your freezer for 20 minutes or until solid. Enjoy!

Per serving: 140 Calories; 15g Fat; 4.9g Carbs; 2g Protein

27. Cocoa Dessert with Almonds

(Ready in about 10 minutes + chilling time | Servings 6)

INGREDIENTS

1/2 stick butter, melted
1/2 teaspoon vanilla paste
10 drops liquid stevia

2 tablespoons cocoa powder
2 tablespoons almonds, chopped

DIRECTIONS

- Melt the butter, vanilla paste, and liquid stevia in a pan that is preheated over a moderate heat.
- Stir in the cocoa powder and stir well to combine.
- Spoon the mixture into 12 molds of a silicone candy mold tray. Scatter the chopped almonds on top. Freeze until set. Enjoy!

Per serving: 84 Calories; 8.9g Fat; 1.5g Carbs; 0.8g Protein

28. Grilled Apples with Star Anise Cream

(Ready in about 15 minutes + chilling time | Servings 4)

INGREDIENTS

Star Anise Cream:
1/2 cup full-fat Greek yoghurt
3 ounces cream cheese
1 cup double cream
2 tablespoons star anise, whole pieces
1/2 teaspoon vanilla paste

Grilled Plums:
2 tablespoons coconut oil
1 cup apples, sliced
1/4 teaspoon ground cloves
1/2 cup pecans, roughly chopped

DIRECTIONS

- Thoroughly combine the full-fat Greek yoghurt and cream cheese with an electric mixer.
- Now, fold in the double cream, star anise, and vanilla paste. Beat until you've reached "soft peak" stage.
- Then, drizzle coconut oil over your apples and cook them on the preheated grill. Sprinkle ground cloves over them and transfer to serving bowls.
- Dollop with chilled cream, garnish with chopped pecans and serve. Enjoy!

Per serving: 312 Calories; 39.4g Fat; 6g Carbs; 5.8g Protein

29. Raspberry Almond Shake

(Ready in about 2 hours | Servings 2)

INGREDIENTS

2 teaspoons instant coffee

4 drops liquid Stevia

1 tablespoon cacao butter

1/4 cup cold water

16 raspberries, frozen

1 cup almond milk

2 tablespoons coconut whipped cream

DIRECTIONS

- Combine the instant coffee, Stevia, cacao butter and cold water. Shake with a drink mixer for 20 seconds.
- Place the frozen raspberries in dessert glasses. Pour the coffee mixture over it. Add the almond milk and ice cubes, if desired.
- Now, freeze for at least 2 hours or until firm. Serve topped with coconut whipped cream. Enjoy!

Per serving: 371 Calories; 37.8g Fat; 5.1g Carbs; 3.4g Protein

30. Cheesecake Fruit Salad

(Ready in about 15 minutes + chilling time | Servings 4)

INGREDIENTS

1 cup blackberries

1 cup raspberries

1/2 cup heavy whipping cream

4 ounces cream cheese, softened at
    room temperature

1 teaspoon liquid Stevia

4 tart cherries, for garnish

DIRECTIONS

- Divide the blackberries and raspberries between four serving bowls.
- Then, whip the heavy cream with the cheese and liquid Stevia until fluffy and well combined.
- Add the whipped cream to the top and serve garnished with cherries. Serve well chilled.

Per serving: 181 Calories; 18.6g Fat; 5.7g Carbs; 2.6g Protein

31. Cream Cheese Coffee Cake

(Ready in about 40 minutes + chilling time | Servings 10)

INGREDIENTS

2/3 cup coconut flour
1 ½ cups almond flour
1/2 teaspoon baking soda
1/2 teaspoon baking powder
A pinch of salt
A pinch of grated nutmeg
1/2 teaspoon Konjac root fiber
1 cup Swerve
1 teaspoon fresh ginger, grated
2 ½ tablespoons ghee
4 eggs

1 cup coconut milk, sugar-free
1 teaspoon rum extract
1 teaspoon vanilla extract

For the Cream Cheese Frosting:
10 ounces cream cheese, cold
1/3 cup powdered granular sweetener
3 ounces butter, at room temperature
1 teaspoon vanilla
A few drops chocolate flavor

DIRECTIONS

- Start by preheating your oven to 360 degrees F. Line a baking pan with parchment paper.
- In a mixing bowl, combine the coconut flour, almond flour, baking soda, baking powder, salt, nutmeg, Konjac root fiber, Swerve, and ginger.
- Microwave the ghee until melted and add to the dry mixture in the mixing bowl. Fold in the eggs, one at a time, and stir until well combined.
- Lastly, pour in the coconut milk, rum extract, and vanilla extract until your batter is light and fluffy.
- Press the mixture into the prepared baking pan. Bake for 28 to 33 minutes or until a cake tester inserted in center comes out clean and dry.
- Let it cool to room temperature.
- Meanwhile, beat the cream cheese with an electric mixer until smooth. Stir in the powdered granular sweetener and beat again. Beat in the vanilla until it is completely incorporated.
- Add the butter, vanilla, and chocolate flavor; whip until light, fluffy and uniform. Frost the cake and serve well-chilled. Bon appétit!

Per serving: 241 Calories; 22.6g Fat; 4.2g Carbs; 6.6g Protein

32. Avocado Mousse with Peanut Butter

(Ready in about 15 minutes | Servings 4)

INGREDIENTS

1 ½ cups avocado, peeled, pitted, and
  diced
1/2 cup crunchy peanut butter
50 drops liquid stevia
1/2 cup canned coconut milk

1 teaspoon pure vanilla extract
1/4 teaspoon ground cloves
1 tablespoon lime juice
1/2 cup coconut whipped cream

DIRECTIONS

- Process the avocados, peanut butter, stevia and coconut milk in a blender.
- Now, add the vanilla extract, cloves, and lime juice.
- Refrigerate until ready serve. Garnish with coconut whipped cream and enjoy!

Per serving: 288 Calories; 28.3g Fat; 4.9g Carbs; 6.2g Protein

33. Waffles with Blueberries and Mascarpone Rum Cream

(Ready in about 20 minutes + chilling time | Servings 8)

INGREDIENTS

Waffles:

Mascarpone Rum Cream:

10 ounces mascarpone cheese, softened

1/4 cup xylitol

1 teaspoon rum extract

1/2 cup double cream

1 cup blueberries

6 eggs

1 stick butter

1/4 cup coconut flour

1 teaspoon baking powder

A pinch of salt

A pinch of ground cinnamon

DIRECTIONS

- Whip the mascarpone cheese until stiff. Add in the xylitol and rum extract.
- In another bowl, whip the double cream until you've reached "soft peak" stage.
- Add the whipped cream to the mascarpone mixture; mix again to combine well. Allow it to cool in your refrigerator for 3 hours.
- Meanwhile, make your waffles. Beat the eggs and butter until creamy and fluffy. Mix in the other ingredients.
- Cook in the preheated waffle iron. Top your waffles with the chilled mascarpone rum cream and serve immediately garnished with blueberries. Bon appétit!

Per serving: 308 Calories; 26.3g Fat; 6g Carbs; 10.7g Protein

34. Easy Chocolate Fudge

(Ready in about 15 minutes + chilling time | Servings 8)

INGREDIENTS

1 cup condensed milk, sugar-free
3/4 Sukrin chocolate, broken into
   pieces
1 stick butter

2 tablespoons coconut oil
4-5 drops Stevia
1/2 cup heavy cream

DIRECTIONS

- Microwave the condensed milk and Sukrin chocolate for 70 seconds; spoon into a baking dish and freeze until firm.
- Melt the butter in a small-sized pan; stir in the melted coconut oil, Stevia, and heavy cream; whisk to combine well or beat with a hand mixer.
- Spread the cream mixture over the fudge layer in the baking dish. Transfer to the refrigerator or freezer until solid. Bon appétit!

Per serving: 220 Calories; 20g Fat; 5g Carbs; 1.7g Protein

35. Holiday Candies with a Boozy Twist

(Ready in about 10 minutes + chilling time | Servings 8)

INGREDIENTS

4 tablespoons butter

4 tablespoons monk fruit

2 ounces cream cheese

4 ounces sugar-free baker's chocolate

2 tablespoons good-quality whiskey

1 teaspoon orange zest

1 teaspoon vanilla essence

Coating:

2 teaspoons monk fruit

2 tablespoons cocoa powder

1 teaspoon cinnamon

DIRECTIONS

- Cream the butter with the monk fruit. Then, fold in the cream cheese and mix again. Microwave the chocolate. Fold in the chocolate and beat until well mixed.
- Add in the whiskey, orange zest and vanilla and mix again.
- Mix the coating ingredients in a shallow bowl. Shape the mixture into balls and roll them over the coating mixture. Enjoy!

Per serving: 172 Calories; 15.7g Fat; 5.4g Carbs; 2.7g Protein

36. Penuche Bars with Walnuts

(Ready in about 2 hours | Servings 8)

INGREDIENTS

1 cup xylitol
1 cup condensed milk, unsweetened
1 stick butter
1/2 teaspoon vanilla paste

2 ounces toasted walnuts, chopped
1/4 teaspoon orange rind, grated
A pinch of salt

DIRECTIONS

- Combine the xylitol and milk in a pan that is preheated over a moderate heat. Simmer, stirring often, for 5 to 6 minutes.
- Stir in the butter and vanilla. Cream with an electric mixer at low speed; beat until very creamy.
- Fold in the chopped walnuts, orange rind, and salt; stir again. Afterwards, spoon into a baking dish and freeze until firm, about 2 hours. Bon appétit!

Per serving: 167 Calories; 18.1g Fat; 5.8g Carbs; 2.4g Protein

37. Restaurant-Style Coconut Pie

(Ready in about 50 minutes | Servings 8)

INGREDIENTS

4 eggs
1 stick butter, melted
1 cup coconut flour
1/2 cup cricket flour
1/2 teaspoon baking powder
A pinch of grated nutmeg
A pinch of ground cloves
1/4 teaspoon ground cinnamon

1/2 cup granulated Swerve
3 whole eggs
1/2 teaspoon coconut extract
1/2 teaspoon vanilla extract
3/4 cup sugar-free caramel syrup
1/3 cup coconut oil, softened
1 teaspoon vanilla extract
1 cup unsweetened coconut, shredded

DIRECTIONS

- Beat the eggs until frothy. Now, fold in the melted butter, flour, baking powder, nutmeg, cloves, cinnamon, and Swerve.
- Mix your dough and form it into a ball. Roll out your dough on a lightly floured surface to fit a pie pan.
- Next, make the filling by mixing the remaining ingredients until everything is well incorporated.
- Spread the filling mixture over the top and cover the top lightly with a piece of foil.
- Bake in the preheated oven at 330 degrees F for 30 minutes. Remove the foil; then, continue baking for 10 to 15 minutes more, being careful not to burn the crust. It should not be overly jiggly. Bon appétit!

Per serving: 324 Calories; 32.4g Fat; 4.2g Carbs; 5.7g Protein

38. Coconut and Chia Dreamsicle Dessert

(Ready in about 20 minutes | Servings 4)

INGREDIENTS

1 cup water

1 cup heavy cream

1 cup coconut milk, unsweetened

1 teaspoon vanilla extract

1 cup chia seeds

1/4 cup coconut shreds, unsweetened

2 tablespoons erythritol

1/4 teaspoon ground cloves

1/2 teaspoon ground anise star

DIRECTIONS

- Thoroughly combine all of the above ingredients in a mixing dish.
- Allow it to stand at least 20 minutes, stirring periodically.
- Divide among four individual cups to serve. Enjoy!

Per serving: 226 Calories; 19.9g Fat; 5g Carbs; 5.9g Protein

39. White Chocolate Fudge Cake

(Ready in about 15 minutes + chilling time | Servings 12)

INGREDIENTS

3/4 cup butter, softened
1 ¼ cups walnut butter, sugar-free
3 ounces sugar-free white chocolate
1/3 cup coconut milk, unsweetened
2 tablespoons xylitol

1/8 teaspoon coarse sea salt
1/4 teaspoon grated nutmeg
1/4 teaspoon ground star anise
1/4 teaspoon lemon peel zest

DIRECTIONS

- Microwave the butter, walnut butter, and white chocolate until they are melted. Add the butter mixture to your food processor.
- Now, add the other ingredients and mix again until everything is well incorporated. Scrape the mixture into a parchment lined baking pan.
- Place in the refrigerator for 3 hours. Cut into squares and serve. Bon appétit!

Per serving: 202 Calories; 21.3g Fat; 2.3g Carbs; 2.4g Protein

40. Cream Cheese and Avocado Pudding

(Ready in about 15 minutes+ chilling time | Servings 6)

INGREDIENTS

1 cup coconut milk

1 ½ cups avocado, pitted, peeled and
   mashed

A pinch of salt

A pinch of grated nutmeg

1 cup heavy cream

1/2 cup softened cream cheese

2 tablespoons confectioners Swerve

DIRECTIONS

- In a deep pan, warm the coconut milk over medium heat.
- Stir in the avocado, salt, and nutmeg and cook, stirring continuously, about 5 minutes or until the mixture bubbles up.
- Then, beat the heavy cream, cheese, and Swerve with an electric mixer on medium-high speed. Reserve roughly 4 tablespoons of this cream mixture to top the mousse before serving.
- Afterwards, place in your refrigerator to set for a couple of hours.
- Serve with a dollop of cream mixture on top. Bon appétit!

Per serving: 303 Calories; 30g Fat; 3.1g Carbs; 3.5g Protein

41. Walnut Brownies with Whipped Cream

(Ready in about 15 minutes+ chilling time | Servings 8)

INGREDIENTS

1 stick butter, at room temperature

3 medium-sized eggs

1/2 teaspoon rum extract

1 teaspoon almond extract

1 cup walnut flour

1 teaspoon baking powder

1/3 cup unsweetened cocoa powder

1/4 teaspoon ground cinnamon

1/4 teaspoon ground cloves

1 cup xylitol

1 cup heavy whipping cream

3 tablespoons granulated Swerve

DIRECTIONS

- In a mixing dish, beat the butter until creamy. Then, fold in the eggs, one at a time and continue beating until they form soft peaks.
- Then, add in the rum extract and almond extract.
- In a separate dish, thoroughly combine the walnut flour, baking powder, cocoa powder, cinnamon, cloves, and xylitol. Now, add the wet ingredients to the dry ingredients and mix well to combine.
- Scrape the batter into a parchment-lined baking pan. Bake in the preheated oven at 360 degrees F for 18 to 20 minutes or until a tester inserted in the middle comes out dry and clean.
- Allow it to cool completely. Now, run a knife around the sides and remove from the baking pan.
- In the meantime, beat the heavy cream with the granulated Swerve. Spread the whipped cream on your brownies and serve well chilled. Bon appétit!

Per serving: 270 Calories; 28.6g Fat; 4.8g Carbs; 4.7g Protein

42. Chocolate Lover's Cookie in a Mug

(Ready in about 10 minutes | Servings 2)

INGREDIENTS

1 tablespoon unsweetened cacao nib

1 ½ ounces cream cheese

2 tablespoons coconut oil, room temperature

1/3 cup almond flour

1/3 teaspoon baking soda

1/4 teaspoon ginger

1/2 teaspoon vanilla essence

1/3 cup xylitol

1 ½ ounces unsweetened baker's chocolate, cut into chunks

DIRECTIONS

- Mix the cacao nib, cream cheese, and coconut oil until creamy and smooth. Mix in the almond flour, baking soda, ginger, vanilla, and xylitol.
- Divide the batter among two mugs. Fold in the chocolate chunks.
- Microwave for about 1 minute 30 seconds or until your cookies are slightly browned on top. Enjoy!

Per serving: 372 Calories; 38.1g Fat; 5.2g Carbs; 6.6g Protein

43. Puffy Strawberry Scones

(Ready in about 25 minutes | Servings 10)

INGREDIENTS

1 cup coconut flour
1 cup almond flour
1 teaspoon baking powder
A pinch of salt
1 cup strawberries

2 eggs
1 ½ sticks butter
1 cup heavy cream
10 tablespoons liquid stevia
1 teaspoon vanilla extract

DIRECTIONS

- Start by preheating your oven to 350 degrees F.
- In a mixing bowl, thoroughly combine the flour with the baking powder, salt and strawberries.
- In another mixing bowl, beat the eggs with the butter and cream. Stir in the liquid stevia and vanilla extract; stir to combine well.
- Combine the 2 mixtures and stir until you obtain a soft dough. Knead gently and avoid overworking your dough.
- Shape into 16 triangles and arrange on a lined baking sheet. Bake for 18 minutes and serve your scones cold.

Per serving: 245 Calories; 24.6g Fat; 4.4g Carbs; 3.8g Protein

44. Coconut Smoothie Bowl with Raspberries

(Ready in about 10 minutes | Servings 4)

INGREDIENTS

1/2 cup raspberries, frozen

1 cup coconut milk

2 tablespoons almond butter

1/4 cup coconut shreds

1 teaspoon vanilla paste

4 drops liquid stevia

2 tablespoons hemp seeds

DIRECTIONS

- Pulse the frozen berries in your food processor to the desired consistency.
- Add the coconut milk, almond butter, coconut, vanilla and stevia. Blend until everything is well incorporated.
- Dived between 4 individual bowls; top with hemp seeds and serve immediately.

Per serving: 274 Calories; 26.8g Fat; 6.1g Carbs; 3.9g Protein

45. Blood Orange Jelly

(Ready in about 10 minutes + chilling time | Servings 10)

INGREDIENTS

1 ½ teaspoons gelatin, unflavored
1 ½ cups coconut milk
1/4 cup erythritol

1 teaspoon Blood orange juice
1 teaspoon blood orange zest

DIRECTIONS

- Place the gelatin and coconut milk in a pan; let it sit for 2 minutes. Add the remaining ingredients.
- Simmer the mixture over low heat until the gelatin is dissolved, about 3 minutes.
- Pour the mixture into 4 molds. Place in your refrigerator until set, at least 6 hours.
- To serve invert over a small plate. Enjoy!

Per serving: 221 Calories; 21.5g Fat; 3.8g Carbs; 4.3g Protein

46. Black Forest Fudge Cake

(Ready in about 1 hour + chilling time | Servings 12)

INGREDIENTS

4 tablespoons almond flour

1/2 teaspoon baking powder

1 tablespoon ground chia seeds

1/2 cup cocoa powder, unsweetened

4 eggs

1 stick butter, melted

1 cup Swerve granular

A pinch of grated nutmeg

1/4 teaspoon ground cloves

1/2 teaspoon ground cinnamon

1 teaspoon vanilla extract

2 tablespoons coconut oil, room temperature

4 ounces sugar-free bakers' chocolate chunks

1/2 cup heavy whipping cream

DIRECTIONS

- In a mixing bowl, thoroughly combine the almond flour, baking powder, chia seeds, and cocoa powder.
- Then, mix in the eggs, butter, Swerve, nutmeg, cloves, cinnamon, and vanilla; mix until everything is well incorporated.
- Scrape the batter into a parchment-lined baking pan. Bake in the preheated oven at 330 degrees F for 50 minutes.
- Add the coconut oil and chocolate chunks to a small-sized saucepan and bring it up to a simmer. Fold in the heavy whipping cream and remove from the heat; stir until everything is well incorporated and glossy. Let it cool completely.
- Spread the cream layer over the brownies and place in your refrigerator until ready to serve. Enjoy!

Per serving: 219 Calories; 19.6g Fat; 4.9g Carbs; 9.4g Protein

47. Almond and Cream Squares

(Ready in about 30 minutes | Servings 8)

INGREDIENTS

2 cups almond flour

3/4 teaspoon baking powder

1/2 cup Swerve

1/2 teaspoon ground cinnamon

A pinch of sea salt

A pinch of grated nutmeg

1 stick butter, melted

3 eggs

1/2 cup Swerve

1 teaspoon vanilla paste

3/4 cup heavy whipping cream

1/2 cup almonds, chopped

DIRECTIONS

- Preheat your oven to 360 degrees F. Then, line a baking pan with parchment paper.
- In a mixing bowl, thoroughly combine the almond flour, baking powder, Swerve, cinnamon, salt, and nutmeg.
- Now, stir in the melted butter, eggs, Swerve, and vanilla paste. Next, stir in the heavy cream to create a soft texture.
- Fold in the chopped almonds and gently stir until everything is well incorporated. Spoon the batter into the baking pan.
- Bake approximately 27 minutes. Allow it to cool completely before serving. Bon appétit!

Per serving: 241 Calories; 23.6g Fat; 3.7g Carbs; 5.2g Protein

48. Creamiest Avocado Custard Ever

(Ready in about 10 minutes + chilling time | Servings 2)

INGREDIENTS

1 egg yolk
1 ½ cups milk
4 tablespoons erythritol
1/2 cup avocado, pitted and mashed

Fresh juice of 1/2 lime
1/2 cup double cream
2 tablespoons cacao powder
1 teaspoon vanilla paste

DIRECTIONS

- In a medium-sized sauté pan, whisk the egg yolk, milk, and erythritol until the erythritol is dissolved and the mixture is smooth. Heat off.
- Mix in the avocado, lime juice, double cream, cacao powder, and vanilla; mix until creamy.
- Pour your custard into a freezer safe dish and freeze for 2 hours. Bon appétit!

Per serving: 440 Calories; 49.2g Fat; 5.3g Carbs; 6.3g Protein

49. Easy Puffy Coconut Cake

(Ready in about 30 minutes | Servings 12)

INGREDIENTS

10 ounces almond meal

1 ounce coconut, shredded

1 teaspoon baking powder

1/8 teaspoon salt

4 eggs, lightly beaten

3 ounces stevia

1/2 stick butter

5 ounces coconut yogurt

5 ounces cream cheese

DIRECTIONS

- Start by preheating your oven to 350 degrees F. Spritz 2 spring form pans with a non-stick cooking spray.
- In a mixing bowl, thoroughly combine the almond meal, coconut and baking powder. Stir in the salt, eggs and 2 ounces of stevia.
- Combine the 2 mixtures and stir until everything is well incorporated.
- Transfer the mixture into 2 spring form pans, introduce in the oven at 350 degrees F; bake for 20 to 25 minutes.
- Transfer to a wire rack to cool completely. In the meantime, mix the other ingredients, including the remaining 1 ounce of stevia.
- Place one cake layer on a plate; spread half of the cream cheese filling over it. Now, top with another cake layer; spread the rest of the cream cheese filling over the top. Bon appétit!

Per serving: 246 Calories; 24.2g Fat; 5.7g Carbs; 8.1g Protein

50. Rich and Easy Almond Frosty

(Ready in about 6 hours | Servings 6)

INGREDIENTS

2 tablespoons butter, melted
20 ounces double cream
1/3 cup powdered erythritol

1/2 teaspoon almond essence
1/2 teaspoon vanilla essence
1/3 cup roasted almonds, crushed

DIRECTIONS

- Whip the butter until fluffy. Now, add in 1/2 of the double cream and continue whipping using a hand mixer on High for about 2 minutes, or until the mixture is thick.
- Mix in the powdered erythritol, almond essence, and vanilla. Fold in the remaining 1/2 of cream.
- Transfer the mixture to a freezer container; top with a piece of wax paper to keep ice crystals from developing.
- Freeze for about 6 hours or until firm. Garnish with almonds just before serving. Enjoy!

Per serving: 440 Calories; 49.2g Fat; 6.3g Carbs; 7.3g Protein

51. Chocolate Almond Bars

(Ready in about 3 hours | Servings 8)

INGREDIENTS

3/4 cup almond butter, sugar-free,
    preferably homemade

1 stick butter

1/3 cup coconut milk

1/4 cup xylitol

1/8 teaspoon salt

1/8 teaspoon grated nutmeg

3 tablespoons xylitol

3 tablespoons butter, melted

1 teaspoon vanilla essence

3 tablespoons cocoa powder

DIRECTIONS

- Microwave the almond butter and regular butter until they melt.
- Add the coconut milk, 1/4 cup xylitol, salt, and nutmeg; stir to combine well and press into a well-greased glass baking dish.
- Refrigerate for 2 to 3 hours or until set.
- In a mixing bowl, make the sauce by whisking 3 tablespoons xylitol, 3 tablespoons of butter melted, vanilla essence and cocoa powder.
- Spread the sauce over your fudge. Cut into squares and store in an airtight container.

Per serving: 180 Calories; 18.3g Fat; 4.5g Carbs; 1g Protein

52. Grandma's Walnut Cheesecake

(Ready in about 1 hour | Servings 14)

INGREDIENTS

8 ounces walnuts, chopped
8 packets stevia
1/4 teaspoon grated nutmeg
A pinch of salt
1/2 cup butter, melted

For the Filling:
22 ounces cream cheese, at room temperature
30 packets stevia
4 eggs
1 teaspoon vanilla essence
1 teaspoon pure almond extract
14 ounces sour cream

DIRECTIONS

- Combine all ingredients for the crust until well mixed; press the crust mixture into a springform pan. Set aside
- Now, beat the cream cheese on low speed until creamy and fluffy.
- Add the stevia and eggs, one at a time; mix on low speed. Add the remaining ingredients until well mixed.
- Bake in the preheated oven at 300 degrees F for 55 minutes. Let it cool on a wire rack. Serve well chilled.

Per serving: 393 Calories; 38g Fat; 4.1g Carbs; 9.8g Protein

53. Chunky Nutty Spring Cookies

(Ready in about 20 minutes | Servings 10)

INGREDIENTS

2 eggs, beaten
1/2 stick butter
1/4 cup sesame butter

4 tablespoons powdered erythritol
1/2 cup roasted peanuts, chopped
1/2 cup roasted almonds, chopped

DIRECTIONS

- Mix all ingredients in a bowl until everything is well incorporated.
- Form the batter into bite-sized balls and arrange them on a parchment-lined cookie sheet; flatten each bowl with a fork or your hands.
- Bake in the preheated oven at 360 degrees F for 12 minutes. Enjoy!

Per serving: 182 Calories; 16.1g Fat; 5.3g Carbs; 5.6g Protein

54. Jaffa Mousse Cake

(Ready in about 15 minutes + chilling time | Servings 6)

INGREDIENTS

2 cups heavy cream

3 tablespoons confectioners Swerve

3 1/3 tablespoons cocoa powder, unsweetened

Fresh juice and zest of 1/2 orange

1/4 teaspoon sea salt

A pinch of grated nutmeg

1/4 teaspoon ground cloves

1/4 teaspoon ground cinnamon

6 ounces sugar-free chocolate chunks

DIRECTIONS

- Whip the heavy cream and Swerve with an electric mixer.
- Add the cocoa powder and beat again. Now, add the remaining ingredients and beat again until everything is well combined.
- Place in your refrigerator until ready to serve. Bon appétit!

Per serving: 158 Calories; 17.7g Fat; 4.2g Carbs; 2.2g Protein

55. Chocolate Hazelnut Bites

(Ready in about 15 minutes + chilling time | Servings 8)

INGREDIENTS

1 stick butter, room temperature

1/4 cup cocoa powder, unsweetened

1/4 cup granulated Swerve

1/2 cup hazelnuts, finely chopped

A pinch of salt

A pinch of ground cloves

DIRECTIONS

- Melt the butter in a pan over a moderate heat. Now, stir in the cocoa powder and Swerve. Heat off and mix well.
- Add the hazelnuts, salt and ground cloves; stir until everything is incorporated.
- Line a baking dish with a piece of aluminum foil. Spoon the mixture into the baking dish and let it sit in your refrigerator until completely set.
- Broken into pieces and serve. Keep in the refrigerator.

Per serving: 184 Calories; 19.9g Fat; 5.2g Carbs; 1.8g Protein

56. Ooey Gooey Lemon Cake

(Ready in about 40 minutes | Servings 8)

INGREDIENTS

Vanilla Layer:

3 eggs

1/3 cup coconut oil, softened

4 tablespoons almond meal

1/2 teaspoon baking powder

1/2 teaspoon baking soda

1/3 cup monk fruit powder

1/4 teaspoon ground star anise

1/4 teaspoon ground cloves

1 teaspoon vanilla essence

Top Layer:

3 eggs

6 ounces Greek yogurt

2 lemons, freshly squeezed

1/3 cup coconut oil, softened

1/3 cup monk fruit powder

DIRECTIONS

- In a mixing bowl, beat the eggs until frothy. Add in the coconut oil and mix again.
- Mix in the remaining ingredients for the vanilla layer. Scrape the mixture into a lightly greased baking pan.
- To make the top layer, in a mixing bowl, beat the eggs until frothy.
- Add in the Greek yogurt, lemon juice, coconut oil, and monk fruit powder; mix until creamy and uniform.
- Pour the lemon mixture on top of the bottom layer. Bake in the preheated oven at 360 degrees F approximately 33 minutes. Bon appétit!

Per serving: 288 Calories; 27.7g Fat; 4.1g Carbs; 7.8g Protein

57. Aromatic Orange Dessert

(Ready in about 1 hour | Servings 5)

INGREDIENTS

3/4 cup Swerve
1 ½ cups whipping cream
3/4 cup water
6 eggs
1 teaspoon orange rind, grated

1/4 teaspoon orange essence
1/2 teaspoon vanilla essence
1/4 teaspoon ground cloves
1 teaspoon star anise star ground

DIRECTIONS

- Melt the Swerve in a pan on medium-low until it is richly browned.
- Spoon the caramelized Swerve into the bottom of a baking dish; set aside.
- Then heat the cream and water in a pan, bringing to a boil.
- In a mixing bowl, whisk the remaining ingredients until everything is well combined. Stir the warm cream mixture into this egg mixture. Cook, stirring frequently, for a further 3 minutes.
- Spread this mixture over the Swerve layer. Place the baking dish in a larger baking pan that is filled with boiling water.
- Bake at 330 degrees F for 1 hour. Invert your pudding onto a serving plate and serve. Bon appétit!

Per serving: 205 Calories; 17.4g Fat; 5.6g Carbs; 7.4g Protein

58. Mini Brownies with Pecans

(Ready in about 25 minutes | Servings 12)

INGREDIENTS

3/4 cup butter, melted

5 eggs

4 ounces cocoa powder

1/2 cup pecans, ground

1 teaspoon vanilla paste

3/4 teaspoon baking powder

1/4 teaspoon ground cloves

3 ounces cream cheese

3 ounces sour cream

2 tablespoons stevia powder

DIRECTIONS

- Preheat your oven to 360 degrees F. Place a baking cup in each of 12 regular-size muffin cups.
- Thoroughly combine all ingredients in your food processor. Spoon the batter into the muffin cups.
- Bake for 18 to 22 minutes. Transfer to a wire rack to cool completely before serving. Bon appétit!

Per serving: 251 Calories; 22.5g Fat; 4.6g Carbs; 6.4g Protein

59. Blackberry Frozen Yogurt

(Ready in about 10 minutes + chilling time | Servings 2)

INGREDIENTS

1/2 cup blackberries, frozen

2 tablespoons sunflower seed butter

1/2 cup plain yogurt

3-4 drops liquid Stevia

A pinch of grated nutmeg

A pinch of ground cinnamon

DIRECTIONS

- Process all of the above ingredients in your blender until well combined.
- Transfer to your freezer or serve right now. Enjoy!

Per serving: 139 Calories; 13.1g Fat; 5.7g Carbs; 7.6g Protein

60. Peanut Candy Bark

(Ready in about 10 minutes + chilling time | Servings 12)

INGREDIENTS

3/4 cup peanut butter

3/4 cup coconut oil

1 cup Swerve

1 teaspoon pure vanilla extract

1/2 teaspoon pure almond extract

1/2 cup coconut flakes

DIRECTIONS

- Combine all ingredients in a pan over a moderate heat; cook, stirring continuously, for 4 to 5 minutes.
- Spoon the mixture into a parchment-lined baking sheet. Refrigerate overnight and break your bark into pieces. Serve.

Per serving: 316 Calories; 31.6g Fat; 4.6g Carbs; 6.6g Protein

61. Whiskey Chocolate Bars

(Ready in about 10 minutes + chilling time | Servings 8)

INGREDIENTS

1 cup chocolate chunks, sugar-free

3 tablespoons cocoa powder

3/4 cup buttermilk

1/2 cup milk

2 tablespoons whiskey

1/4 teaspoon grated nutmeg

1/8 teaspoon ground cloves

1/8 teaspoon cinnamon powder

1/2 teaspoon vanilla paste

DIRECTIONS

- Melt the chocolate, along with the cocoa and buttermilk in a microwave-safe bowl, on high for 70 seconds.
- Stir in the other ingredients. Pour the mixture into silicone molds.
- Refrigerate at least 1 hour 30 minutes. Bon appétit!

Per serving: 90 Calories; 6.4g Fat; 5.1g Carbs; 2.4g Protein

62. Avocado and Cappuccino Popsicles

(Ready in about 10 minutes + chilling time | Servings 8)

INGREDIENTS

1 ½ cups avocado, pitted, peeled and mashed

1 cup brewed espresso

2 tablespoons cocoa powder

1 cup heavy whipping cream

3 tablespoons erythritol

1/2 teaspoon cappuccino flavor extract

A pinch of salt

A pinch of grated nutmeg

DIRECTIONS

- Throw all of the above ingredients into your food processor; mix until everything is well combined.
- Pour the mixture into an ice cube tray. Freeze overnight, at least 6 hours. Serve well-chilled.

Per serving: 117 Calories; 12.2g Fat; 5g Carbs; 1.3g Protein

63. Cheesecake Mousse Fluff

(Ready in about 10 minutes + chilling time | Servings 5)

INGREDIENTS

5 ounces cream cheese, at room temperature

1/3 cup cocoa butter

A pinch of salt

1/3 cup erythritol

1/4 teaspoon ground star anise

1 cup double cream

Almond Brittle:

4 tablespoons coconut oil, at room temperature

1/4 cup granulated Swerve

1/2 cup almonds, toasted and slivered

DIRECTIONS

- Beat the cream cheese with the cocoa butter until firm. Stir in the salt, erythritol and star anise.
- Fold in the cream and mix to combine. Divide between dessert bowls and transfer to your refrigerator until ready to serve.
- Then, melt the coconut oil in a small sauté pan over moderate heat. Add in the Swerve and continue stirring until it has dissolved completely.
- Heat off and fold in the almonds. After that, spread the mixture in an even layer on a parchment-lined cookie sheet. Allow the almond brittle to cool completely; then, refrigerate until firm.
- Serve on top of the cheesecake mousse fluff and enjoy!

Per serving: 423 Calories; 44.7g Fat; 3.7g Carbs; 4.6g Protein

64. Silky Dark Chocolate Bars

(Ready in about 25 minutes + chilling time | Servings 10)

INGREDIENTS

1/2 cup coconut flour
1 cup almond flour
2 packets stevia
1/4 teaspoon cardamom
1/2 teaspoon star anise, ground
1/2 teaspoon coconut extract
1 teaspoon pure vanilla extract

1 tablespoon rum
A pinch of table salt
1/2 stick butter, cold
1 ½ cups double cream
8 ounces bittersweet chocolate chips, sugar-free

DIRECTIONS

- Preheat an oven to 330 degrees F. Now, line a baking dish with parchment paper.
- Add the flour, stevia, cardamom, anise, coconut extract, vanilla extract, rum and salt to your food processor. Blitz until everything is well combined.
- Cut in the cold butter and process to combine again.
- Press the batter into the bottom of the prepared baking dish. Bake about 13 minutes; transfer to a wire rack to cool slightly.
- To make the filling, bring the double cream to a simmer in a pan. Add the chocolate and whisk until uniform. Spread over the crust; cut into squares and serve well-chilled. Enjoy!

Per serving: 119 Calories; 11.7g Fat; 5.2g Carbs; 1.1g Protein

65. Apple Crumb Cake with Coconut

(Ready in about 30 minutes | Servings 8)

INGREDIENTS

2 ½ cups apples, cored and sliced

1/2 tablespoon fresh lemon juice

1/3 teaspoon xanthan gum

1 cup almond flour

1/4 cup coconut flour

3/4 cup xylitol

2 eggs, whisked

5 tablespoons coconut oil, melted

DIRECTIONS

- Start by preheating your oven to 360 degrees F. Lightly grease a baking dish with a non-stick cooking spray.
- Arrange the apples on the bottom of the baking dish. Drizzle with lemon juice and xanthan gum.
- Then, in a mixing bowl, mix the flour with xylitol and eggs until the mixture resembles coarse meal. Spread this mixture over the apples.
- Drizzle coconut oil over the topping. Bake for 25 minutes or until the dough rises. Bon appétit!

Per serving: 152 Calories; 13.8g Fat; 4.7g Carbs; 2.5g Protein

66. Walnut Rum Biscotti

(Ready in about 35 minutes | Servings 12)

INGREDIENTS

1 stick butter

1 egg yolk

1 whole egg

1/3 cup coconut milk

1/3 cup Monk fruit powder

1 teaspoon rum extract

1/4 cup flax seed meal

1/2 cup coconut flour

1/3 teaspoon baking powder

1/3 cup ground walnuts

DIRECTIONS

- Cream the butter and eggs for a few minutes; then, mix in the coconut milk, Monk fruit powder, and rum extract.
- Fold in the flax seed meal, coconut flour, baking powder, and ground walnuts; mix to combine well.
- Scrape the mixture into a parchment-lined cookie sheet; bake in the preheated oven at 360 degrees F for about 28 minutes, until they are crisp. Bon appétit!

Per serving: 109 Calories; 12.1g Fat; 1.3g Carbs; 1.4g Protein

67. Creamy Chia Pudding Parfaits

(Ready in about 30 minutes | Servings 4)

INGREDIENTS

1/3 cup chia seeds

1/2 cup water

1 cup coconut cream

1/2 cup sour cream

1/3 teaspoon vanilla extract

1 teaspoon key lime zest

1/4 teaspoon ground cinnamon

2 tablespoons granular Swerve

DIRECTIONS

- In a bowl, place all ingredients and stir well; let it sit at least 30 minutes.
- Divide among individual bowls to serve.
- Can be stored in the refrigerator up to 3 days.

Per serving: 270 Calories; 25.7g Fat; 4.5g Carbs; 4.6g Protein

68. Vanilla and Lemon Delight

(Ready in about 1 hour | Servings 6)

INGREDIENTS

3 avocados, pitted, peeled and mashed

1 tablespoon vanilla extract

1 cup xylitol

1/8 teaspoon xanthan gum

1 teaspoon lemon juice

1 cup buttermilk

1 cup full-fat milk

DIRECTIONS

- Mix all ingredients in your blender or a food processor.
- Refrigerate for 1 hour before serving. Enjoy!

Per serving: 248 Calories; 20.8g Fat; 5g Carbs; 4.6g Protein

69. Velvety Cream Cake

(Ready in about 30 minutes + chilling time | Servings 10)

Per serving: 211 Calories; 19g Fat; 4.4g Carbs; 7g Protein

INGREDIENTS

For the Crust:

4 tablespoons peanut butter, room temperature

1 cup almond meal

2 tablespoons almonds, toasted and chopped

For the Filling:

10 ounces cream cheese, room temperature

2 eggs

1/2 teaspoon Stevia

1/2 teaspoon vanilla essence

1/2 teaspoon sugar-free caramel flavored syrup

1 teaspoon fresh ginger, grated

A pinch of salt

A pinch of grated nutmeg

DIRECTIONS

- Begin by preheating your oven to 360 degrees F. Line a baking pan with parchment paper.
- Thoroughly combine the peanut butter with the almond meal. Then, press the crust mixture into your baking pan and bake for 7 minutes.
- Then, make the filling, by mixing all the filling ingredients with an electric mixer.
- Spread the filling onto the prepared crusts; bake for a further 18 minutes.
- Transfer it to the refrigerator to chill. Garnish with chopped, toasted almonds; cut into squares and serve well-chilled. Bon appétit!

70. Chocolate Rum Kisses

(Ready in about 15 minutes + chilling time | Servings 7)

INGREDIENTS

2 tablespoons almond milk

A pinch of flaky sea salt

A pinch of grated nutmeg

1/4 teaspoon ground cinnamon

1/4 teaspoon ground cardamom

2 ounces coconut butter

3 ounces sugar-free dark chocolate
   chunks

4 tablespoons xylitol

2 tablespoons rum

1/2 teaspoon pure almond extract

DIRECTIONS

- Whisk the almond milk with the salt, nutmeg, cinnamon, and cardamom.
- Microwave the coconut butter and chocolate; stir into the milk mixture and mix to combine well.
- After that, add in the xylitol, rum, and pure almond extract; mix again.
- Spoon the mixture into silicone molds and allow them to cool completely. Enjoy!

Per serving: 148 Calories; 13.1g Fat; 3.7g Carbs; 1.9g Protein

71. Brandy Balls with Walnuts

(Ready in about 1 hour | Servings 10)

INGREDIENTS

1/2 stick butter

4 ounces heavy cream

1/4 cup Sukrin Icing

1 tablespoon brandy

1/2 teaspoon pure almond extract

1/2 cup chopped toasted walnuts

1/2 cup chocolate chips, sugar-free

4 tablespoons walnuts, coarsely
   chopped

DIRECTIONS

- Melt the butter in a double boiler, stirring constantly.
- Then, stir in the cream and Sukrin icing; stir to combine well. Remove from the heat and add the brandy, almond extract and chopped walnuts.
- Now, allow it to cool at room temperature. Shape into 20 balls and chill for 40 to 50 minutes.
- In a double boiler, melt the chocolate chips over medium-low heat. Dip each ball into the chocolate coating.
- Afterwards, roll your balls in chopped walnuts. Keep in an airtight container in your refrigerator. Enjoy!

Per serving: 162 Calories; 18.6g Fat; 4.9g Carbs; 2.3g Protein

72. Chocolate Rolls with Pistachios

(Ready in about 25 minutes + chilling time | Servings 6)

INGREDIENTS

3 bars sugar-free chocolate spread
1/2 cup heavy cream
1 teaspoon vanilla essence

1/4 teaspoon ground cinnamon
1/2 cup toasted pistachios, finely
   chopped

DIRECTIONS

- Melt the chocolate spread with the heavy cream in your microwave for 1 minute or so.
- Add the vanilla and ground cinnamon; transfer to your refrigerator for 8 hours or until firm enough to shape.
- Shape the chocolate mixture into balls. Freeze for 20 minutes.
- Afterwards, roll the balls into the chopped pistachios. Keep refrigerated until ready to serve.

Per serving: 113 Calories; 8.5g Fat; 4.9g Carbs; 1.7g Protein

73. Fudgesicles Fudge Pops

(Ready in about 10 minutes + chilling time | Servings 8)

INGREDIENTS

1/2 cup full-fat coconut milk
1/2 teaspoon agar agar
8 ounces coconut cream

3 tablespoons unsweetened cocoa
1 tablespoon monk fruit liquid

DIRECTIONS

- Warm the coconut milk in a saucepan and gradually stir in agar agar; mix to combine.
- Heat off. Fold in the coconut cream, cocoa, and monk fruit liquid; mix with an electric mixer until everything is creamy and smooth.
- Divide among popsicle molds, add the popsicle sticks and freeze for 1 hour. Allow your fudgesicles to thaw slightly before unmolding and serving. Enjoy!

Per serving: 133 Calories; 13.6g Fat; 3.9g Carbs; 1.8g Protein

74. Decadent Butterscotch Dessert

(Ready in about 15 minutes + chilling time | Servings 8)

INGREDIENTS

3/4 cup heavy cream
1/2 cup coconut milk
1 tablespoon butterscotch flavoring
25 drops liquid stevia

1/3 teaspoon pure vanilla extract
A pinch of salt
1/4 cup sour cream

DIRECTIONS

- Cook the heavy cream and coconut milk in a pan that is preheated over a medium-low flame. Let it simmer, stirring constantly, until there are no lumps.
- Allow it to cool at room temperature; mix in the remaining ingredients.
- Blend with an electric mixer until your desired consistency is reached. Transfer to your freezer for about 5 hours. Enjoy!

Per serving: 99 Calories; 11.3g Fat; 1.5g Carbs; 0.8g Protein

75. Peanut Butter Cupcakes

(Ready in about 40 minutes | Servings 10)

INGREDIENTS

1/2 cup coconut oil

1/2 cup butter

1/2 cup crunchy peanut butter

3 tablespoons heavy cream

1 tablespoon granular Swerve

DIRECTIONS

- Simmer all of the above ingredients in a pan over medium-low heat; stir continuously until everything is well incorporated.
- Divide the batter among muffin cups lined with cupcake wrappers.
- Allow them to harden at least 30 minutes in your freezer. Bon appétit!

Per serving: 266 Calories; 28.1g Fat; 2.6g Carbs; 3.3g Protein

Made in the USA
Middletown, DE
14 September 2019